Flavors of India A Comprehensive Guide to Authentic Indian Recipes

INDIAN RECIPES

CHEF's life

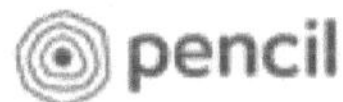 pencil

ISBN 978-93-5883-105-4
© CHEF's life 2023

Published in India 2023 by Pencil

A brand of
One Point Six Technologies Pvt. Ltd.
Unit no. 26, Ground Floor, Building A1,
Wadala Truck Terminal Road,
Near Post Office, Antop Hill, Mumbai - 400037
E connect@thepencilapp.com
W www.thepencilapp.com

DISCLAIMER: *The opinions expressed in this book are those of the authors and do not purport to reflect the views of the Publisher.*

Author biography

AN engineer

CONTENTS

Preface

Welcome to "Flavors of India: A Comprehensive Guide to Authentic Indian Recipes." This book is a heartfelt ode to the rich tapestry of Indian cuisine, which boasts a kaleidoscope of flavors, colors, and aromas. With its diverse regional variations and culinary traditions, Indian cooking is a delightful amalgamation of ancient techniques, age-old recipes, and a myriad of spices.

India's culinary heritage is a reflection of its vibrant history, a melting pot of cultures, and a celebration of local ingredients. From the bustling streets of Mumbai to the tranquil backwaters of Kerala, each region of India has its unique culinary identity, leaving a lasting impression on anyone fortunate enough to indulge in its delectable offerings.

In this comprehensive guide, we present a collection of 35 authentic Indian recipes that will take you on a journey of exploration through the culinary wonders of India. Whether you are an experienced chef or a novice cook, these step-by-step recipes have been meticulously crafted to ensure that you can recreate the magic of Indian flavors in your own kitchen.

Within these pages, you will discover the art of blending spices to create the perfect balance of taste, the secrets of making fluffy bread straight from the tandoor, and the joy of savoring mouth-watering street food that has delighted generations. From tantalizing appetizers and hearty main courses to decadent desserts and refreshing beverages, this book is a treasure trove of culinary delights that cater to every palate.

Beyond the recipes themselves, we have endeavored to capture the essence of Indian cooking—the sense of community that emerges when families gather around the dinner table, the nostalgia evoked by the aroma of familiar spices, and the joy of sharing meals with loved ones.

As you embark on this gastronomic adventure through the flavors of India, we hope that you not only discover new recipes but also gain a deeper appreciation for the cultural significance of food in India. May this book inspire you to embrace the joy of cooking, create cherished memories, and explore the rich heritage of Indian cuisine.

So, put on your apron, gather your ingredients, and let's embark on this delightful culinary journey together. The kitchen awaits, filled with the promise of a delightful experience that will linger in your heart long after the last morsel has been savored.

Happy cooking and bon appétit!

With warmest regards,

Author, "Flavors of India: A Comprehensive Guide to Authentic Indian Recipes"

Chapter 1 Introduction to Indian Cuisine

An overview of the rich culinary heritage, regional diversity, and essential cooking techniques.

Chapter 2 Spices and Seasonings

A detailed guide to commonly used Indian spices and their unique flavors.

Chapter 3 Chutneys and Dips

3.1 Mint Coriander Chutney Procedure:

A refreshing green chutney made with fresh mint, coriander, and spices.

3.2 Tamarind Chutney Procedure:

A sweet and tangy chutney made with tamarind, dates, and jaggery.

Chapter 4 Appetizers and Street Food

4.1 Samosas Procedure:

Crispy pastry pockets filled with spiced potatoes and peas.

4.2 Pakoras Procedure:

Deep-fried fritters made with various vegetables and chickpea flour batter.

Chapter 5 Chaats

5.1 Bhel Puri Procedure:

A delightful combination of puffed rice, vegetables, and chutneys.

5.2 Dahi Puri Procedure:

Hollow puris filled with spiced yogurt and chutneys.

Chapter 6 Soups and Salads

6.1 Mulligatawny Soup Procedure:

A hearty lentil and vegetable soup with a South Indian twist.

6.2 Kachumber Salad Procedure:

Fresh and colorful salad made with cucumbers, tomatoes, and onions.

Chapter 7 Main Course - Vegetarian Delights

7.1 Palak Paneer Procedure:

Soft paneer (cottage cheese) cooked in a creamy spinach gravy with spices.

7.2 Baingan Bharta Procedure:

Roasted eggplant mash sautéed with onions, tomatoes, and spices.

Chapter 8 Main Course - Non-Vegetarian Delights

8.1 Butter Chicken Procedure:

Succulent pieces of chicken cooked in a rich and creamy tomato-based sauce.

8.2 Fish Curry Procedure:

Fish fillets simmered in a flavorful coconut-based gravy.

Chapter 9 Biryanis and Rice Dishes

9.1 Vegetable Biryani Procedure:

Fragrant basmati rice cooked with vegetables, aromatic spices, and saffron.

9.2 Chicken Biryani Procedure:

A classic biryani preparation with marinated chicken and fragrant rice.

Chapter 10 Dals and Lentils

10.1 Dal Makhani Procedure:

Slow-cooked black lentils and kidney beans in a creamy tomato gravy.

10.2 Tadka Dal Procedure:

Yellow lentils tempered with spices and garnished with a tadka of ghee and cumin seeds.

Chapter 11 Breads and Accompaniments

11.1 Naan Procedure:

Soft and fluffy leavened bread, best served with curries and kebabs.

11.2 Roti/Chapati Procedure:

Whole wheat unleavened flatbread, a staple in Indian households.

Chapter 12 Regional Specialties

12.1 Chole Bhature Procedure:

Spicy and tangy chickpea curry served with deep-fried bread (bhature).

12.2 Dhokla Procedure:

Steamed savory gram flour cakes, a specialty of Gujarat.

Chapter 13 Street Food Favorites

13.1 Pav Bhaji Procedure:

A popular Mumbai street food dish with spicy vegetable curry served with buttered buns.

13.2 Aloo Tikki Procedure:

Crisp potato patties served with chutneys and toppings.

Chapter 14 Breakfast Delights

14.1 Masala Dosa Procedure:

Thin, crispy crepes made from fermented rice and lentil batter, filled with spiced potato masala.

14.2 Poha Procedure:

Flattened rice stir-fried with vegetables and spices, a quick and light breakfast option.

Chapter 16 Tandoori Specials

16.1 Tandoori Chicken Procedure:

Marinated chicken roasted in a tandoor for a smoky and flavorful taste.

16.2 Tandoori Paneer Tikka Procedure:

Spiced and marinated paneer skewers, cooked to perfection in a tandoor.

Chapter 17 Side Dishes

17.1 Bhindi Masala Procedure:

Okra stir-fried with onions, tomatoes, and spices for a delicious side dish.

17.2 Aloo Gobi Procedure:

A classic combination of potatoes and cauliflower cooked with spices.

Chapter 18 Indian Sweets and Desserts

18.1 Gulab Jamun Procedure:

Soft and syrup-soaked milk-solid dumplings, a quintessential Indian dessert.

18.2 Kheer Procedure:

Creamy rice pudding flavored with cardamom and garnished with nuts.

Chapter 19 Drinks and Beverages

19.1 Masala Chai Procedure:

Spiced Indian tea brewed with milk and aromatic spices.

19.2 Mango Lassi Procedure:

A refreshing and creamy mango yogurt drink, perfect for hot summer days.

Chapter 20 Festive Delicacies

20.1 Rasgulla Procedure:

Soft and spongy cottage cheese dumplings served in sugar syrup, a festive treat.

20.2 Coconut Barfi Procedure:

Sweet and coconutty fudge made with condensed milk, a popular festival sweet.

Chapter 21 Diwali Specials

21.1 Diwali Namakpare Procedure:

Savory and crispy diamond-shaped snacks seasoned with spices.

21.2 Kaju Katli Procedure:

Delicate cashew fudge flavored with saffron and garnished with edible silver foil.

Chapter 22 Indian Pickles and Preserves

22.1 Lemon Pickle Procedure:

Tangy and spicy lemon pickle made with lemons, spices, and oil.

22.2 Mixed Vegetable Pickle Procedure:

A medley of vegetables marinated with spices and preserved in oil.

Chapter 23 Condiments and Spice Mixes

23.1 Garam Masala Procedure:

A fragrant and warm spice blend used to enhance various dishes.

23.2 Chaat Masala Procedure:

Tangy and savory spice mix used in chaats and street food.

Chapter 24 Fusion Creations

24.1 Butter Chicken Pizza Procedure:

A fusion of classic Indian butter chicken flavors with pizza.

24.2 Curry Spiced Pasta Procedure:

Indian-inspired pasta dish with a curry twist.

Chapter 25 One-Pot Meals

25.1 Vegetable Pulao Procedure:

Fragrant and flavorful rice dish cooked with mixed vegetables and spices.

25.2 Khichdi Procedure:

Comforting and nourishing one-pot meal made with rice, lentils, and vegetables.

Chapter 26 Regional Bread Varieties

26.1 Makki Ki Roti Procedure:

Traditional Punjabi cornmeal flatbread served with Sarson ka Saag.

26.2 Puri Procedure:

Puffed deep-fried bread that pairs well with spicy curries.

Chapter 27 Rajasthani Delicacies

27.1 Dal Baati Churma Procedure:

A traditional Rajasthani meal comprising lentil curry, baked wheat balls (baati), and sweet churma.

27.2 Gatte ki Sabzi Procedure:

Gram flour dumplings cooked in a flavorful yogurt-based gravy.

Chapter 28 South Indian Specialties

28.1 Sambar Procedure:

Tangy and spicy lentil stew with vegetables, served with idli or dosa.

28.2 Avial Procedure:

Mixed vegetable curry with coconut and yogurt, a South Indian delight.

Chapter 29 Bengali Cuisine

29.1 Fish Curry with Mustard Paste Procedure:

A quintessential Bengali fish curry made with mustard seeds and spices.

29.2 Mishti Doi Procedure:

Sweetened yogurt delicacy, a favorite dessert in Bengal.

Chapter 30 Gujarati Thali

30.1 Undhiyu Procedure:

A mixed vegetable curry cooked with a blend of spices, a part of the traditional Gujarati thali.

30.2 Dhokla Procedure:

Steamed gram flour cakes, a popular Gujarati snack.

Chapter 31 Mughlai Delights

31.1 Mutton Korma Procedure:

A rich and creamy Mughlai curry made with tender mutton and aromatic spices.

31.2 Shahi Tukda Procedure:

A royal Mughlai dessert made with fried bread soaked in sweetened milk.

Chapter 32 Indo-Chinese Fusion

32.1 Gobi Manchurian Procedure:

Cauliflower florets coated in a spicy and tangy sauce, a popular Indo-Chinese dish.

32.2 Vegetable Fried Rice Procedure:

Flavorful fried rice cooked with vegetables and Chinese sauces.

Chapter 33 Coastal Cuisine

33.1 Goan Prawn Curry Procedure:

A delectable prawn curry from Goa, known for its coconut-based gravy.

33.2 Kerala Fish Moilee Procedure:

Fish cooked in a creamy and mildly spiced coconut milk gravy.

Chapter 34 Awadhi Cuisine

34.1 Galouti Kebab Procedure:

Melt-in-your-mouth kebabs made with minced meat and aromatic spices.

34.2 Lucknowi Biryani Procedure:

Fragrant and flavorful biryani from Lucknow, known for its tender meat and rich taste.

Chapter 35 Sweets from Across India

35.1 Rasmalai Procedure:

Soft and spongy cottage cheese dumplings served in flavored milk, a popular sweet.

35.2 Besan Ladoo Procedure:

Sweet and nutty gram flour ladoos, a favorite during festive occasions.

Enjoy the delightful journey of cooking and savoring authentic Indian flavors with these detailed recipes!

Chapter 15 Regional Curries

15.1 Vindaloo Procedure:

Spicy and tangy Goan curry made with meat or vegetables, vinegar, and red chilies.

15.2 Kadhi Procedure:

Yogurt-based curry with gram flour dumplings, a comfort food in North India.